Shoot for the Moon

Even if you miss you will land among the stars.

HAZELDEN®
Keep Coming Back™

Created by Meiji Stewart

Illustrated by David Blaisdell

Shoot for the Moon
© 1996 by Meiji Stewart

ISBN# 1-56838-380-0

Hazelden
P.O. Box 176
15251 Pleasant Valley Road
Center City, MN 55012-0176
1-800-328-9000
www.hazelden.org

Illustration: David Blaisdell, Tucson, Arizona
Cover design: Kahn Design, Encinitas, California

Dedicated to:
My beautiful wife and best friend, Claudia. My daughter, Malia
and my step-son, Tommy. My mother, Nannette, and father,
Richard, my sister, Leslie, my brothers, Ray and Scott, my
nephews and nieces Sebastien, Emilie, Skye, Luke, Jake,
Nannette, Cairo and Kamana, and to Julie, Tom, Fumi,
Jocelyne, Richard and Stephen.

Thanks to:
David for the wonderful illustrations. I am blessed to be able to
work with him. Thanks also to Roger, Gita, and Darryl for
putting it all together, almost always under deadline (usually
yesterday). Thanks to Jeff for the delightful book covers, and,
even more, for his and Pete's friendship. Thanks to Gay, Jane,
Regina, Rich, Neill, and Zane for making it possible to bring
these gift books to life. And thanks to my mom and dad for
encouraging me to pursue my dreams.

Why not go out on a limb?
Isn't that where the fruit is?

Frank Scully

When you believe you can –
you can!

Maxwell Maltz

Even if you're on the right track,
you'll get run over if you just sit there.

Will Rogers

Take a chance! All life is a chance.
The person who goes farthest is generally
the one who is willing to do and dare.
The "sure thing" boat never gets far from shore.

Dale Carnegie

And will you succeed?
Yes indeed, yes indeed!
Ninety-eight and three-quarters percent guaranteed!

Dr. Seuss

One doesn't discover new lands
without consenting to lose sight
of the shore for a very long time.

André Gide

I have never lost a game in my life.
Once in a while, time ran out on me.

Bobby Lane

You can either take action, or you can
hang back and hope for a miracle.
Miracles are great, but they are so unpredictable.

Peter Drucker

Care, thought, and study go into
making something succeed; luck is
something you get playing in the
lottery, a roulette game, or gambling.

Wes Roberts

People can rain on your parade
only if you let them.

Knock the "t" off "can't."

George Reeves

Sow a thought and you
reap an act;
Sow an act and you
reap a habit;
Sow a habit and you
reap a character;
Sow a character and you
reap a destiny.

Samuel Smiles

People are always blaming their
circumstances for what they are.
I don't believe in circumstances.
The people who get on in this world
are the people who get up and look
for circumstances they want; if they
can't find them, they make them.

George Bernard Shaw

What we vividly imagine,
ardently desire,
enthusiastically act upon,
must inevitably come to pass.

Colin P. Sisson

You miss 100% of the shots you never take.

Wayne Gretsky

Shoot for the moon.
Even if you miss, you
will land among the stars.

Until one is committed there is
hesitancy, the chance to draw back,
always ineffectiveness.Concerning
all acts of initiative (and creation) is
one elemental truth; that the
moment one definitely commits
oneself, then Providence moves too.

Johann Wolfgang von Goethe

If you wait for the perfect moment when all is safe and assured, it may never arrive. Mountains will not be climbed, races won, or lasting happiness achieved.

Maurice Chevalier

Do the thing you fear,
and the death of fear is certain.

Ralph Waldo Emerson

He who attracts luck carries with
him the magnet of preparation.

William Ward

I never did anything worth
doing by accident, nor did any of
my inventions come by accident;
they came by work.

Thomas Edison

If you don't make a total commitment
to whatever you're doing,
then you start looking to bail out the
first time the boat starts leaking.
It's tough enough getting that boat to
shore with everybody rowing,
let alone when a guy stands up and
starts putting his jacket on.

Lou Holtz

If I have the belief that I can do it,
I shall surely acquire the capacity to do it,
even if I may not have it
at the beginning.

Mahatma Gandhi

If you have built castles in the air,
your work need not be lost;
that is where they should be.
Now put foundations under them.

Henry David Thoreau

If you can't stand the heat,
stay out of the kitchen.

Harry S. Truman

Failure is delay, but not defeat.
It is a temporary detour, not
a dead-end street.

William Arthur Ward

Happiness Is...

Adventures in self discovery

Being true to yourself

Creating a life you love

Disposition not circumstance

Enjoying what you have

Finding balance

Growing friendships

Having someone to love

an **I**nside job, go within

a **J**ourney of the heart

Knowing when to let go

Learning from your mistakes

Making the best of any situation

Not taking things personally

Optional, so is misery

Progress not perfection

the **Q**uality of your thoughts

Reverence for body, mind and spirit

Spending time with loved ones

Today well lived

Unconditional, no if's and's or but's

Valuing feelings and needs

Whatever makes your heart sing

Xpressing your truth lovingly

Your choice, if not now, when?

Zzzzzzz's, a good night's sleep

© Meiji Stewart

43

Forget your opponents.
Always play against par.

Sam Snead

If there is a book you really want to read, but it hasn't been written yet, then you must write it.

Toni Morrison

Don't wait for your
ship to come in;
swim out to it.

One may not reach the dawn save
by the path of the night.

Kahlil Gibran

Expect the best.
Convert problems into opportunities.
Be dissatisfied with the status quo.
Focus on where you want to go,
instead of where you're coming from.
Decide to be happy; knowing it's an attitude,
a habit gained from daily practice,
and not a result or payoff.

Dennis Waitley

Ulcers are something you
get from mountain climbing
over molehills.

When you get to the end of your rope,
tie a knot, hang on, and swing.

Leo Buscaglia

I will study and get ready, and
maybe my chance will come.

Abraham Lincoln

The great composer does not set to work
because he is inspired, but becomes
inspired because he is working.
Beethoven, Wagner, Bach, and Mozart
settled down day after day to the job in
hand with as much regularity as an
accountant settles down each day to his
figures. They didn't waste time
waiting for inspiration.

Ernest Newman

What counts most is not
necessarily the size of
the dog in the fight,
but the the size of the
fight in the dog.

Dwight D.Eisenhower

It's a funny thing about life;
if you refuse to accept anything but
the best, you very often get it.

W. Somerset Maugham

If a man can write a better book,
preach a better sermon,
or make a better mousetrap
than his neighbor,
though he build his
house in the woods,
the world will make a
path to his door.

Ralph Waldo Emerson

Genius
is one percent inspiration, and
ninety-nine percent perspiration.

Thomas Edison

The credit belongs to the man who is actually in the arena; whose face is marred by dust and sweat and blood; who strives valiantly; who errs and comes short again and again; who knows the great enthusiasms, the great devotions, and spends himself in a worthy cause; who, at the best, knows in the end the triumph of high achievement; and who, at the worst, if he fails, at least fails while daring greatly, so that his place shall never be with those cold and timid souls who know neither victory nor defeat.

Theodore Roosevelt

Do not follow where the
path may lead.
Go instead where there is no
path and leave a trail.

If you don't do your homework,
you won't make your free throws.

Larry Bird

Life shrinks or expands in
proportion to one's courage.

Anais Nin

To try is to risk failure.
But risk must be taken, as
the greatest hazard in life is to
risk nothing. The person who
risks nothing, does nothing,
has nothing, and is nothing.

Everyone has talent.
What is rare is the courage
to follow the talent
to the dark place where it leads.

Erica Jong

If you ain't the lead dog,
the scenery never changes.

Lewis Grizzard

Don't despair; it's often the last key
of the bunch that opens the door.

The door of opportunity won't open
unless you do some pushing.

A little neglect may breed great mischief...
For want of a nail, the shoe was lost;
for want of a shoe, the horse was lost;
for want of a horse, the battle was lost;
for want of the battle, the war was lost.

Benjamin Franklin

Plan ahead.
It was not raining when
Noah built the ark.

Two men look out through the same bars;
one sees the mud, and one the stars.

Frederick Langbridge

We are what we repeatedly do.
Excellence, then, is not
an act, but a habit.

Aristotle

No age or time of life,
no position or circumstance,
has a monopoly on success.
Any age is the right age to start doing.

Progress always involves risks.
You can't steal second base and
keep your foot on first.

James Bryant Conant

Learn to listen.
Opportunity could be knocking at
your door very softly.

Frank Tyger

A shortcut is often the quickest way
to some place you weren't going.

Nothing worthwhile ever
happens quickly and easily.
You achieve only as you are
determined to achieve...and as you
keep at it until you have achieved.

Robert H. Lauer

Keep on going and the chances are that you will stumble on something, perhaps when you are least expecting it. I have never heard of anyone stumbling on something sitting down.

Charles F. Kettering

Perserverence is a great element of success.
If you only knock long enough and
loud enough at the gate,
you are sure to wake up somebody.

Henry Wadsworth Longfellow

Eighty percent of success is just
showing up.

Woody Allen

Try?
There is no try.
There is only do or not do.

Yoda

Preparation is rarely easy
and never beautiful.

Maya Angelou

Don't be afraid to take a
big step if one is indicated.
You can't cross a chasm
in two small jumps.

David Lloyd George

Nothing will ever be attempted
if all possible objections must first
be overcome.

Samuel Johnson

Everybody is a genius,
just on different subjects.

Did you ever hear of a man who
had striven all his life faithfully and
singly toward an object, and in no
measure obtained it?
If a man constantly aspires, is
he not elevated?

Henry David Thoreau

All things are possible.
Pass it on.

Barbara Milo Ohrbach

Obstacles are those frightful things you see
when you take your eyes off the goal.

Hannah Moore

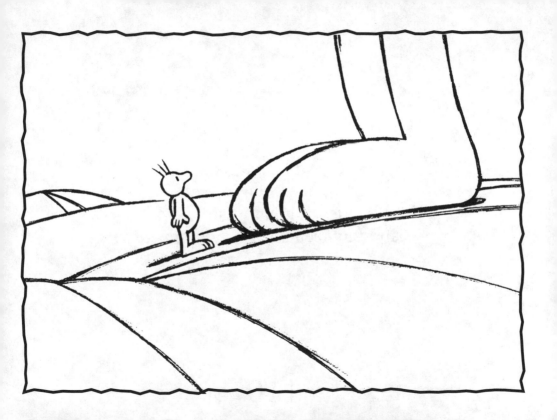

Give a man a fish,
and you feed him for a day;
teach him to fish,
and you feed him for a lifetime.

He who would learn to fly one day
must first learn to stand and walk
and run and climb and dance;
one cannot fly into flying.

Friedrich Nietzsche

I have not failed.
I've discovered one thousand
ways not to build a light bulb.

Thomas Edison

Having the world's best idea will do
you no good unless you act on it.
People who want milk shouldn't sit on
a stool in the middle of a field in
hopes that a cow will back up to them.

Curtis Grant

If at first you don't succeed —
try reading the instructions.

Some of us are more capable
than others of us,
but none of us are more
capable than all of us.

Nothing in the world can take the place of perseverance. Talent will not; nothing is more common than unsuccessful men with talent. Genius will not; unrewarded genius is almost a proverb. Education will not; the world is full of educated failures. Persistence and determination alone are omnipotent.

Calvin Coolidge

I am a great believer in luck,
and I find the harder I work,
the more I have of it.

Stephen Leacock

A journey of a thousand miles
begins with the first step.

Lao-Tsu

There are no limits to what we can do.
The only limits there are, are the
ones we put on ourselves.

The greatest discovery of my generation is that a human being can alter his life by altering his attitudes.

William James

126

I know of no more encouraging
fact than the unquestionable
ability of man to elevate his life
by conscious endeavor.

Henry David Thoreau

Are you in earnest? Then
seize this very minute.
What you can do, or dream
you can, begin it;
Boldness has genius, power
and magic in it;
only engage and then the
mind grows heated;
Begin, and then the work
will be completed.

J.W. von Goethe

You can't hit a home run unless you step up to the plate.

Kathy Seligman

When you get into a tight place,
and everything goes against you,
till it seems as if you could not go on a
minute longer, never give up then,
for that's just the place and the time
that the tide will turn.

H. B. Stowe

I Am...

Amazing, the architect of my destiny.

Beautiful, both inside and out.

Courageous, willing to take chances.

Dynamic, ever changing and growing.

Enthusiastic, about living and loving life.

Fallible, perfectly imperfect.

Grateful, for each and every day.

Healthy, full of energy.

Intuitive, looking within for answers.

Joyful, grateful for all that is.

Kindhearted, reaching out to others.

Lovable, exactly as I am.

Miraculous, a child of the universe.

Now here, fully in this moment.

Optimistic, anything is possible.

Powerful, beyond imagination

Quick, to build bridges not walls.

Resourceful, obstacles are stepping stones

Spiritual, having a human experience.

Trustworthy, speaking from the heart.

Unique, and unrepeatable.

Valuable, I make a difference.

Wise, open to all of life's lessons.

Xcited, about living and loving life.

Young At Heart, delightfully childlike.

Zestful, happy to be me!

Do just once what others say you can't do, and you will never pay attention to their limitations again.

Edmund Brown, Jr.

The most absurd and reckless
aspirations have sometimes led to
extraordinary success.

Vauvenargues

The man who removes a mountain
begins by carrying away small
stones.

Chinese proverb

The moment you commit and quit holding back, all sorts of unforeseen incidents, meetings and material assistance will rise up to help you. The simple act of commitment is a powerful magnet for help.

Napolean Hill

What isn't tried won't work.

Claude McDonald

You are one of a kind; therefore, no one can really predict to what heights you might soar. Even you will not know until you spread your wings!

Gil Atkinson

The heights by great men reached and kept
Were not attained by sudden flight,
But they, while their companions slept,
Were toiling upward in the night.

Henry Wadsworth Longfellow

Look at a stone cutter hammering away at his rock, perhaps a hundred times without as much as a crack showing in it. Yet at the hundred-and-first blow it will split in two, and I know it was not the last blow that did it, but all that had gone before.

Jacob A. Riis

There are no shortcuts to
any place worth going.

Beverly Sills

It is only the farmer who faithfully
plants seeds in the spring,
who reaps a harvest in the autumn.

B. C. Forbes

I always remember an epitaph which is in the cemetery at Tombstone, Arizona. It says: "Here lies Jack Williams. He done his damnedest." I think that is the greatest epitaph a man can have – when he gives everything that is in him to do the job he has before him. That is all you can ask of him and that is what I have tried to do.

Harry S. Truman

The best picture has not yet been painted;
the greatest poem is still unsung;
the mightiest novel remains to be written;
the divinest music has not been
conceived even by Bach.
In science, probably ninety-nine percent
has not yet been discovered.

Lincoln Steffens

If one advances confidently in
the direction of his dreams,
and endeavors to live his life
which he has imagined,
he will meet success
unexpected in common hours.

Henry David Thoreau

Little gift books, big messages

8313

6608

6457

6456

6460

Little gift books, big messages

6458

6568

6569

6566

6570

About the Author

Meiji Stewart has created other gift books, designs, and writings that may be of interest to you. Please visit www.puddledancer.com or call 1-877-EMPATHY (367-2849) for more information about any of the items listed below.

(1) **Keep Coming Back** - Over two hundred gift products including greeting cards, wallet cards, bookmarks, magnets, bumper stickers, gift books, and more. (Free catalog available from Hazelden at 800-328-9000.)

(2) **ABC Writings** - Titles include *Children Are, Children Need, Creativity Is, Dare To, Fathers Are, Friends Are, Grandparents, Great Teachers, Happiness Is, I Am, Life Is, Loving Families, May You Always Have, Mothers Are, Recovery Is, Soulmates, Success Is,* and many more works in progress. Many of these ABC writings are available as posters (from Portal Publications) at your favorite poster and gift store, or directly from Hazelden on a variety of gift products.

(3) *Nonviolent Communication: A Language of Compassion* by Marshall Rosenberg. (from PuddleDancer Press) - Jack Canfield (*Chicken Soup for the Soul* author) says, "I believe the principles and techniques in this book can literally change the world – but more importantly, they can change the quality of your life with your spouse, your children, your neighbors, your co-workers, and everyone else you interact with. I cannot recommend it highly enough." Available from Hazelden and your local and on-line bookstores. For more information about The Center for Nonviolent Communication please visit www.cnvc.org.

◼ HAZELDEN®
Keep Coming Back™

Complimentary Catalog Available
Hazelden: P.O. Box 176, Center City, MN 55012-0176
1-800-328-9000   www.hazelden.org

Hazelden/Keep Coming Back titles available from your favorite bookstore:

Relax, God is in Charge	ISBN 1-56838-377-0
Keep Coming Back	ISBN 1-56838-378-9
Children are Meant to be Seen and Heard	ISBN 1-56838-379-7
Shoot for the Moon	ISBN 1-56838-380-0
When Life Gives You Lemons…	ISBN 1-56838-381-9
It's a Jungle Out There!	ISBN 1-56838-382-7
Parenting… Part Joy… Part Guerrilla Warfare	ISBN 1-56838-383-5
God Danced the Day You Were Born	ISBN 1-56838-384-3
Happiness is an Inside Job	ISBN 1-56838-385-1
Anything is Possible	ISBN 1-56838-386-X

Acknowledgements

Every effort has been made to find the copyright owner of the material used.
However, there are a few quotations that have been impossible to trace, and we
would be glad to hear from the copyright owners of these quotations, so that
acknowledgement can be recognized in any future edition.

Hazelden Information and Educational Services is a division of the Hazelden Foundation, a not-for-profit organization. Since 1949, Hazelden has been a leader in promoting the dignity and treatment of people afflicted with the disease of chemical dependency.

The mission of the foundation is to improve the quality of life for individuals, families, and communities by providing a national continuum of information, education, and recovery services that are widely accessible; to advance the field through research and training; and to improve our quality and effectiveness through continuous improvement and innovation.

Stemming from that, the mission of this division is to provide quality information and support to people wherever they may be in their personal journey—from education and early intervention, through treatment and recovery, to personal and spiritual growth.

Although our treatment programs do not necessarily use everything Hazelden publishes, our bibliotherapeutic materials support our mission and the Twelve Step philosophy upon which it is based. We encourage your comments and feedback.

The headquarters of the Hazelden Foundation is in Center City, Minnesota. Additional treatment facilities are located in Chicago, Illinois; New York, New York; Plymouth, Minnesota; St. Paul, Minnesota; and West Palm Beach, Florida. At these sites, we provide a continuum of care for men and women of all ages. Our Plymouth facility is designed specifically for youth and families.

For more information on Hazelden, please call **1-800-257-7800.** Or you may access our World Wide Web site on the Internet at **www.hazelden.org.**